bubblefacts...

GREAT INVENTIONS

Miles Kelly

PUBLISHING

First published in 2004 by
Miles Kelly Publishing Ltd
Bardfield Centre, Great Bardfield, Essex, CM7 4SL

Copyright © Miles Kelly Publishing Ltd 2004

2 4 6 8 10 9 7 5 3 1

Editorial Director:
Anne Marshall

Senior Editor:
Belinda Gallagher

Editorial Assistant:
Lisa Clayden

Designer:
Debbie Meekcoms

Cartoons:
Mark Davis

Production:
Estela Boulton

ISBN 1–84236–436–7

Printed in China

British Library Cataloguing-in-Publication Data
A catalogue record for this book is available from the British Library

Indexer: Jane Parker

www.mileskelly.net
info@mileskelly.net

Contents

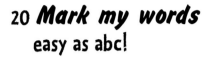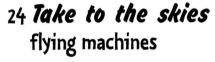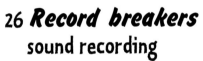

Tools
of the trade
stone and flint

People have been inventors for thousands of years. Our ancient relatives began inventing more than 400,000 years ago by making stone tools such as axes. These early people hammered stone with stone to make rough shapes and some of these tools have been found in Tanzania in Africa. Scientists call this ancient relative 'handy man'.

People used reindeer antlers to dig for flint, a kind of stone. It was chipped to make sharp tools and weapor

Some Stone Age hunters threw boomerangs! They were made from mammoth tusks, and used for hunting animals.

Stone Age saws could cut through the strongest wood. Flint workers discovered how to make small flint flakes. They fixed the flakes like teeth into a straight piece of wood or bone. If the teeth broke they could add new ones. The first flint saws were made about 12,000BC.

FLAMIN' FLINT GETS EVERYWHERE!

HERE'S ONE I MADE EARLIER...

ER, THAT'S NOT A SAW!

Woolly mammoths were hunted with flint-tipped spears. Saws with flint teeth easily cut through wood.

Round and round

wonderful wheels!

Over 5000 years ago, the Sumerian people of Mesopotamia invented wheels made from carved planks. They discovered they could move heavy loads easily, when previously they would have been dragged, sometimes on sledges. These first wheels were held together by metal rims.

People soon realized that wheels could be attached to wooden carts to make moving loads easier.

Ancient Egyptians used lighter spoked wheels. Metal train wheels weren't invented until 1789.

In 1861, bikes called boneshakers had solid tyres. Modern trucks with huge wheels can compete in shows.

Magic metal

good as gold!

People found gold and copper in the ground around 8000BC. Early metal workers from the eastern Mediterranean used stone to beat the copper and gold into weapons and ornaments. Around 8500 years ago, bellows made of animal skins were used to blow air onto flames, which could then melt metal out of ores (rocks). We call this 'smelting'.

Bronze was made 5500 years ago by smelting copper and tin ores together. Bronze made stronger weapons.

can you believe it?

Stone Age people invented the first refrigerators! They buried spare food in pits dug in ground that was frozen.

Metal workers discovered iron by adding charcoal to fires instead of wood. A charcoal fire burns much hotter than an ordinary wood fire. This extra heat was good for smelting iron. Weapons made from iron were stronger than those made from bronze.

TEMPER TEMPER!

WELL THAT'S THROWN A SPANNER IN THE WORKS...

WELL DONE BOYS, THE EMPEROR CAN HAVE A BATH.

Iron, a strong metal, was discovered around 1500BC. Lead water pipes were invented by the ancient Romans.

Sail into the sunset

ship ahoy!

The first boats were simple log rafts and were used to transport loads. These were very slow. Sails were invented 5000 years ago, and they really speeded things up. Viking explorers made fast boats with both sails and oars, and 1000 years ago Viking explorers reached America.

Viking longboats travelled far across the oceans. But by the 1700s huge sailing ships ruled the waves.

About 300 years ago sailing ships sailed all the world's oceans. Some, like the British man-of-war fighting ships, were enormous, with many sails and large crews of sailors. Countries such as Britain, France, Spain and Holland had huge navies made up of these ships.

In 450BC a merchant called Himilco sailed from North Africa to Britain. He ended up in Cornwall and bought Cornish tin!

PIRATES! LET 'EM HAVE IT!

CHEEK! WE'RE RESPECTABLE NAVAL OFFICERS!

THAT'S TAKEN THE WIND OUT OF THEIR SAILS!

WHOOOSH! BANG!

ZOOOM!

Modern sailing boats have machines to roll up the sails, and gears that allow the boat to steer itself.

Plotting a path

finding a way

Early sailors used the stars to find their way. They noticed that the stars were in certain positions in the sky. By 1735 the chronometer was used as a clock at sea, specially mounted to remove the effect of a ship's motion. The sextant helped sailors work out where they were by measuring the height of the Sun from the horizon.

By using the stars, merchants from Syria were able to sail out of sight of land without getting lost.

The compass was invented in China 3000 years ago. A German, Martin Behain, invented the globe in 1492.

Maps, chronometers and sextants are still used. Today, satellites send signals to help us find our way.

Time after time... ...after time!

Time can be measured in many ways. One of the earliest clocks was a stick in the ground, invented by the Egyptians. The length of the shadow it cast showed the time of day. Candles, water and sand have all been used too. Perhaps the biggest 'calendar' is the great stone slabs at Stonehenge in England, which were built between 3000 and 1550BC.

Some stones at Stonhenge were arranged to line up with sunrise on the longest day of the year.

Some clocks look like birds. Swiss cuckoo clocks contain a bird on a spring that flies out of a door and 'cuckoos' the time.

Stonehenge was built by skilled Bronze Age engineers. Some of the massive stones were somehow brought to the site from a quarry in Wales about 385 kilometres away! They were arranged in such a way that the sun shone into the entrance on the morning of the summer solstice – the longest day of the year.

DON'T BE SUCH A DRIP!

WELL... I'M BOILING A BIG EGG!

I KNOW IT'S NOT **QUITE** TOP-OF-THE-RANGE QUARTZ CRYSTAL...

By 1656, clocks depended on movement, and Dutchman Christiaan Huygens invented the swinging pendulum.

Power of nature

wind and water

Natural energy from the Earth has been used for centuries. The first inventions to use wind power were sailing boats used by the Egyptians and Sumerians around 3500BC. Windmills for grinding grain were first used in AD600.

Can you believe it?

The earliest steam engine was invented by a 3rd century Greek engineer.

SSSSWISH!

TURN IT UP A BIT MATE, I'M RUNNING LATE!

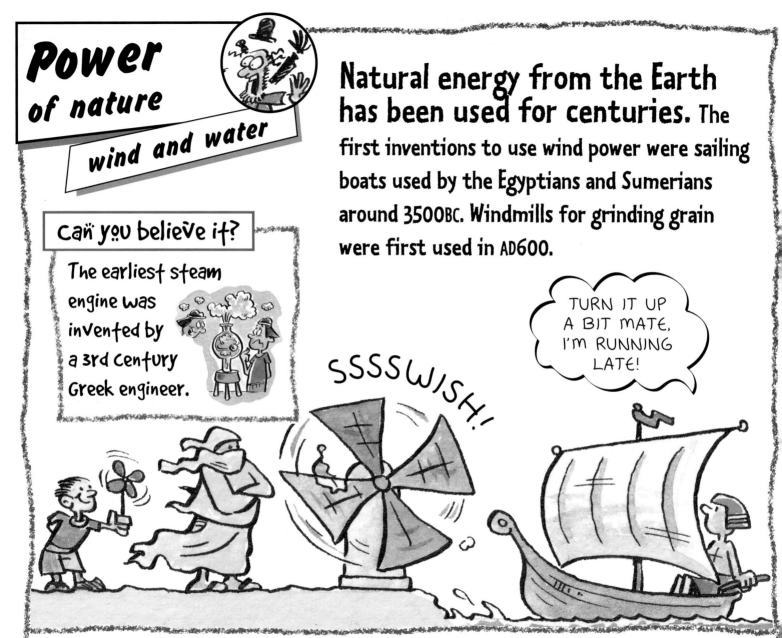

Arab countries first used windmills. The first sailing boats just had a single square sail.

Romans waterwheels were used to grind grain around 100BC. Steam power was first used in the 1600s.

Faraday discovered an electric current created by spinning magnets, which lead to the electric motor.

Making flames

the coming of fire

The first fire users lived in Africa more than 250,000 years ago. Fire helped people keep warm and provided heat for cooking food. The first fires were created by lightning, but people discovered how to make fire by placing a loop of bowstring around a stick and moving the bow quickly back and forth.

People invented lamps to light deep dark caves. The lamps were saucers of clay or stone that burned animal fat, with moss used for a wick. Campfire flames also kept wild animals away at night and gave people light to make cave paintings.

Rubbing a bowstring around a stick created heat, and eventually smoke, then fire

Making fire by rubbing sticks took time. By chipping flint on metal, people found they could make sparks.

fire provided light to make cave paintings

food cooked on a fire was tastier and safer to eat

Fire made food such as roots and meat taste good. Cooking also killed germs and made food safer to eat.

Mark my words

easy as abc!

The first writing was made up of pictures. Writing was invented by the Sumerians 5500 years ago. They scratched their writing onto clay tablets. The most famous picture-writing is the hieroglyphics of the ancient Egyptians, from about 5000 years ago.

The first-ever book came from Egypt between 1500 and 1350BC. It was called 'The Book of the Dead'.

Christian monks wrote on animal skins until Gutenberg invented the printing press in the 15th century.

Written numbers were used in 3100BC. The abacus, a frame with beads, followed. Computers are faster!

Keep in touch!

it's good to talk

People communicate in many ways. Native Americans used smoke signals that were visible from miles away. Some African tribes used 'talking drums'. Before electrical inventions such as the telephone, sending long-distance messages had to be simple.

The certain beat of drums gave tribes information. Lowering and raising blankets broke smoke into signals

Early TV pictures were so fuzzy, performers had to wear thick, clownlike make-up so viewers could see their faces!

Wooden arms on tall poles sent signals hundreds of kilometres in 18th-century France. Claude Chappe invented this system, now called semaphore, in 1797. Until recently, navies used semaphore flags to signal from ship to ship.

BUZZ OFF!

TAP TAP! TAP TAP!

I'M FLAGGING!

HALLO? HALLO? THESE PLASTIC CUPS ARE GREAT!

IDIOT!

In 1838 Samuel Morse invented a code that could be tapped along a wire. Telephones arrived in the 1870s.

Take to the skies

flying machines

Long before they could, people had dreamed of flying. The French Montgolfier brothers invented a hot-air balloon in 1782. The first passengers were a sheep, a duck and a cockerel. Fires on board were common as the hot air that inflated the balloon was created by burning straw and wool!

The first aircraft flight lasted 12 seconds, when the Wright brothers flew their plane in 1903.

The British Royal Airforce Aerobatic team was formed in 1965. They became known as the Red Arrows. This team of Hawk jets needs perfect timing to perform their close formation flying at high speed.

In 1783 the first hydrogen balloon was attacked by a team of terrified farm workers when it landed.

DARNED FEARTHERS!

ZZOOOM!!

OOH LA LA!

The jet engine was invented in 1930, and in 1948 a jet plane flew faster than the speed of sound.

Record breakers

sound recording

The first sound recording was of the nursery rhyme 'Mary had a little lamb'. In 1877 Thomas Edison recorded sounds by making scratch marks on a cylinder tube with a needle. Moving the needle over the marks again repeated the sounds. Today, lots of music can be recorded onto a single lightweight CD.

To play the first discs, a handle had to be turned. Emile Berlin invented disc recording in 1887.

The first photograph was taken in 1826. In 1888, early films had to be watched through a hole in a box.

The Lumière brothers invented the movie projector in 1895. Today, lasers 'read' coded sounds on CDs.

Time-saving gadgets are great to use. The first vacuum cleaner was invented in 1902 by Englishman Cecil Booth. It was so big that it had to be moved by a horse and cart! The first electric 'Hoover' was built from a wooden box, an electric fan and an old sack in 1907 in America.

Early vacuum cleaners worked by opening and closing bellows. The electric version arrived in 1907.

Flushing toilets were used in Crete 4000 years ago.
In 1885 Thomas Twyford invented the first all-china flushing toilet.

A melted chocolate bar lead to the invention of the microwave oven. In 1953, American Percy L. Spencer noticed that a microwave machine where he worked had melted the chocolate in his pocket. In a microwave oven, microwaves make food heat itself up from the inside. A generator produces microwaves that are deflected onto food on a rotating tray.

WHAT'S THAT TERRIBLE PONG?

LIGHT OF MY LIFE!

THANKS!

Early refrigerators were large, noisy and smelly. Air-tight light bulbs were invented in 1929.

From Earth into space
super speed!

THREE...TWO...
ONE...BLAST-OFF!

A jet airliner once flew at twice the sound of speed! *Concorde* could race through the skies at an incredible 2150 kilometres an hour. It carried passengers in luxury across the Atlantic at a fraction of the usual air crossing time – under 3 hours. It cruised at a height of 18,000 metres. *Concorde* stopped flying in 2003.

GOES LIKE...

WWHOOSH!

vVVVRROOOM!

...A ROCKET!

CHEAT

The Chinese invented gunpowder. They used it in rockets in the 13th century to defeat a mongol army.

The space shuttle travels on a giant fuel tank with side rockets into space. Then the tank and rockets drop away and the shuttle circles the Earth at a height of 241 kilometres. American scientists invented the reusable shuttle, which first flew into space in 1981.

Can you believe it?

A 15th-century Chinaman called Wan Hu tried to make a flying machine out of 47 rockets and two kites!

Apollo 11 landed the first men on the Moon in 1969. They were Neil Armstrong and Buzz Aldrin.

Index